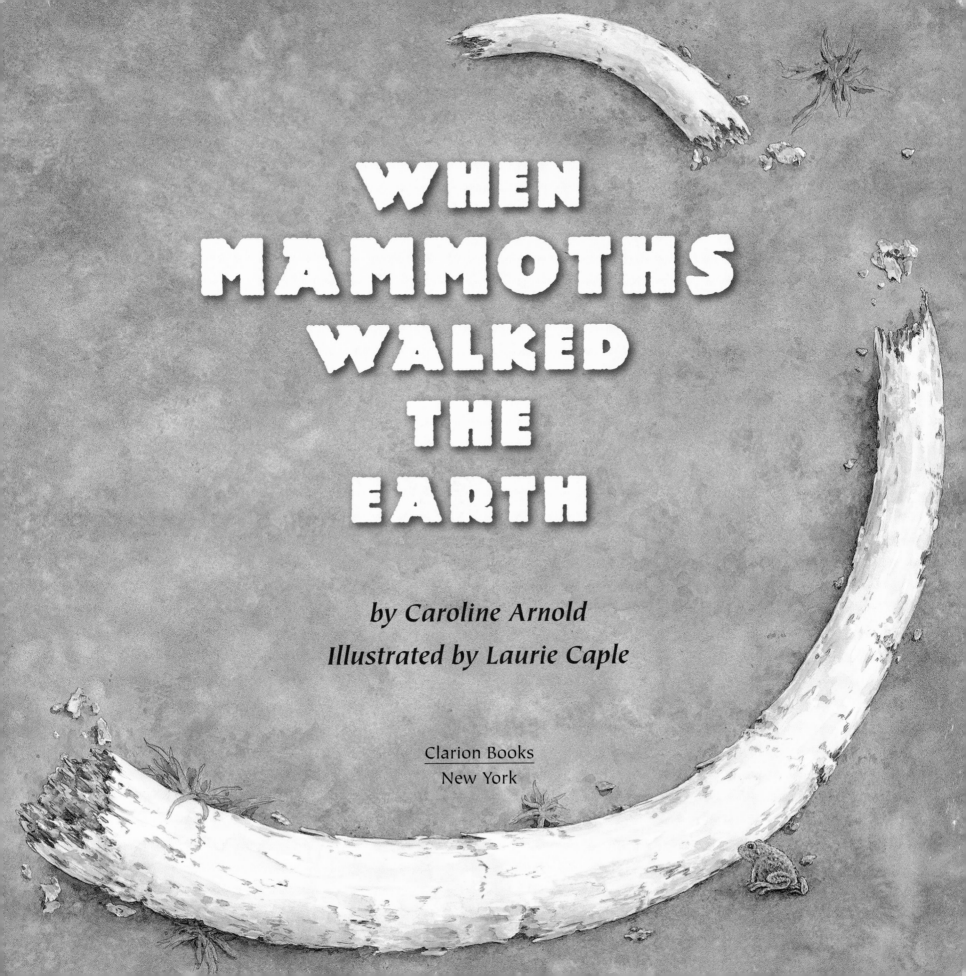

WHEN MAMMOTHS WALKED THE EARTH

by Caroline Arnold

Illustrated by Laurie Caple

Clarion Books

New York

To Jan and Dave Loring
—L.C.

Acknowledgments

I would like to thank Dr. John M. Harris, Chief Curator, the George C. Page Museum, Los Angeles, California, for his expert advice and reading of the manuscript.
—C.A.

I am indebted to Dr. Larry Agenbroad, Professor of Geology at Northern Arizona University, Flagstaff, and Site Director of the Mammoth Site of Hot Springs, South Dakota, for his expert advice on how best to depict mammoths and their world. Special thanks to the knowledgeable staffs at the Mammoth Site of Hot Springs, South Dakota, and at the Ice Age Exhibit, Smithsonian National Museum of Natural History, Washington, D.C.
—L.C.

Clarion Books
a Houghton Mifflin Company imprint
215 Park Avenue South, New York, NY 10003
Text copyright © 2002 by Caroline Arnold
Illustrations copyright © 2002 by Laurie Caple

The text was set in 14-point Tiepolo Book.
The illustrations were executed in watercolor.

For information about permission to reproduce selections from this book, write to Permissions, Houghton Mifflin Company, 215 Park Avenue South, New York, NY 10003.

www.houghtonmifflinbooks.com

Printed in Singapore.

Library of Congress Cataloging-in-Publication Data
Arnold, Caroline.
When mammoths walked the earth / by Caroline Arnold ; illustrated by Laurie Caple.
p. cm.
Includes index.
Summary: Describes the physical characteristics, known habits, and fossil sites of mammoths, prehistoric animals closely related to the elephant.
ISBN 0-618-09633-7
1. Mammoths—Juvenile literature. [1. Mammoths. 2. Prehistoric animals. 3. Paleontology.]
I. Caple, Laurie A., ill. II. Title.
QE882.P8 A76 2002
569'.67—dc21   2001047192

TWP 10 9 8 7 6 5 4 3 2 1

CONTENTS

GIANTS OF THE ICE AGE

About 26,000 years ago, toward the end of the last Ice Age, hungry Columbian mammoths descended the steep sides of a large sinkhole near what is now the town of Hot Springs, South Dakota, to feed on green plants growing at the bottom. The sides of the sinkhole were slippery, and many of the huge animals found it impossible to climb out again. They perished, and as dirt and rocks eroded into the hole, their bones became buried. In 1974, a bulldozer operator preparing land for a building project uncovered the giant bones. Since then, this fossil site, which includes the remains of at least one hundred mammoths, has been helping to provide new information about these huge extinct animals.

Mammoths were once common throughout much of the northern hemisphere, roaming as far north as the Arctic Circle. Prehistoric people were familiar with these large animals. They painted and carved them in caves and on rock walls, engraved their images on small slabs of stone and pieces of bone and ivory, and carved them as figurines. Prehistoric art, archaeological evidence, and fossil remains are helping us to learn more about mammoths. People have unearthed mammoth bones in places ranging from gravel pits and coal mines to tar pits and the bottom of the sea. Whole bodies of mammoths have been discovered frozen in ice, with features such as skin color, hair, and even the remains of the animal's last meal preserved intact. From these and other discoveries we are learning more about the appearance and behavior of mammoths and what the world was like when they were alive.

The Ice Age

The Ice Age, or Pleistocene (PLICE-toe-seen) epoch, began about 1.8 million years ago and lasted until about 10,000 years ago. During much of this time the northern parts of the Earth were covered with huge sheets of ice. So much of the Earth's water was frozen that the sea level was at times nearly three hundred feet lower than it is today and a land bridge connected what is now Siberia and Alaska. The Pleistocene was actually a series of ice ages with long stretches of cold, lasting thousands of years, interrupted by shorter periods, called interglacials, when the climate was somewhat warmer. The last of these cold periods was from about 10,000 to 100,000 years ago and is often called the last Ice Age. The Earth is currently in an interglacial period.

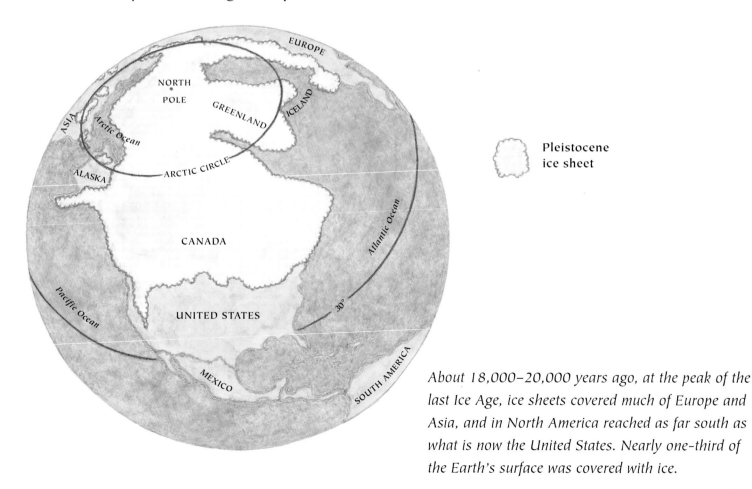

Pleistocene
ice sheet

About 18,000–20,000 years ago, at the peak of the last Ice Age, ice sheets covered much of Europe and Asia, and in North America reached as far south as what is now the United States. Nearly one-third of the Earth's surface was covered with ice.

Many large animals, including mammoths, giant elk, woolly rhinos, giant beavers, and other species that are now extinct, thrived in the Pleistocene.

Woolly mammoth

Giant elk

Giant beaver

Woolly rhinoceros

Sabertooth cat

7

THE FIRST MAMMOTHS

The earliest mammoths lived in Africa about 4–5 million years ago. Between 2.5 and 3 million years ago some of the mammoths migrated from Africa to Europe. They became a species called *Mammuthus meridionalis* (MAM-uh-thus meh-RID-ee-oh-nal-is). These mammoths slowly spread across Europe and Asia and eventually reached North America soon after the beginning of the Ice Age.

About one million years ago, during a period when the climate was cooling, the northern forests where the mammoths lived were becoming grasslands. Like other animals that inhabited these regions, the mammoths had to adapt to their changing world. In northern Europe and Asia the *Mammuthus meridionalis* species became the steppe mammoth, or *Mammuthus trogontherii* (troh-gon-THAIR-ee-ee). The steppe mammoths were the largest mammoths that ever lived, reaching heights of more than fourteen feet. They were the ancestors of the woolly mammoths, or *Mammuthus primigenius* (prime-ih-JEN-ee-us).

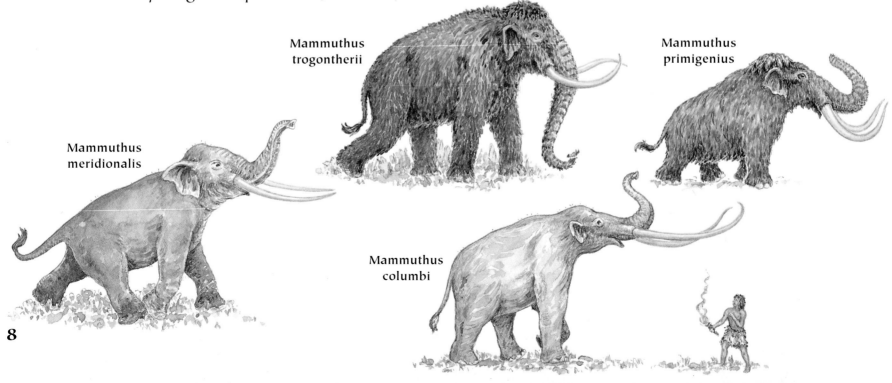

Mammuthus
trogontherii

Mammuthus
primigenius

Mammuthus
meridionalis

Mammuthus
columbi

In North America, *Mammuthus meridionalis* became a different species known as the Columbian mammoth, or *Mammuthus columbi* (koh-ʟᴜᴍ-bee). Variations in the size and characteristics of Columbian mammoth specimens and different methods of naming and classifying fossils have led to the use of several names for this species. In some cases, they are called the Imperial mammoth, *Mammuthus imperator* (im-ᴘᴀʀᴇ-uh-tore), and in others, Jefferson's mammoth, *Mammuthus jeffersonii* (jeff-ur-ѕᴏʜɴ-ee-ee). As scientists continue to study mammoth fossils, they will better understand the true relationship between the various specimens and their classification.

Both the woolly mammoths and Columbian mammoths survived to the end of the Ice Age and were the species known to prehistoric humans.

Mᴀᴍᴍᴜᴛʜᴜѕ ᴍᴇʀɪᴅɪᴏɴᴀʟɪѕ was a forest dweller that ate grass and the leaves and fruit of trees and shrubs. Adults grew about thirteen feet high and weighed about ten tons.

MAMMOTHS AND THEIR RELATIVES

Mammoths are close cousins to the elephants and share a distant ancestor. They form a group that scientists call the Elephantidae (el-eh-FAN-tuh-die). Members of this group share many features, including sturdy bodies, long trunks, ridged molar teeth, and tusks made of solid dentine. (Dentine is the hard material underneath the enamel of your teeth.) Elephants are not the descendants of mammoths, but because they are so closely related, our knowledge of these living animals is helping us to learn about the ancient mammoths. Elephants, for instance, mature slowly and have long life spans. Females and their young typically live in family groups, while adult males are solitary. Individuals communicate both by body movements and by making deep rumbling sounds. It is likely that mammoths behaved in similar ways.

African elephants

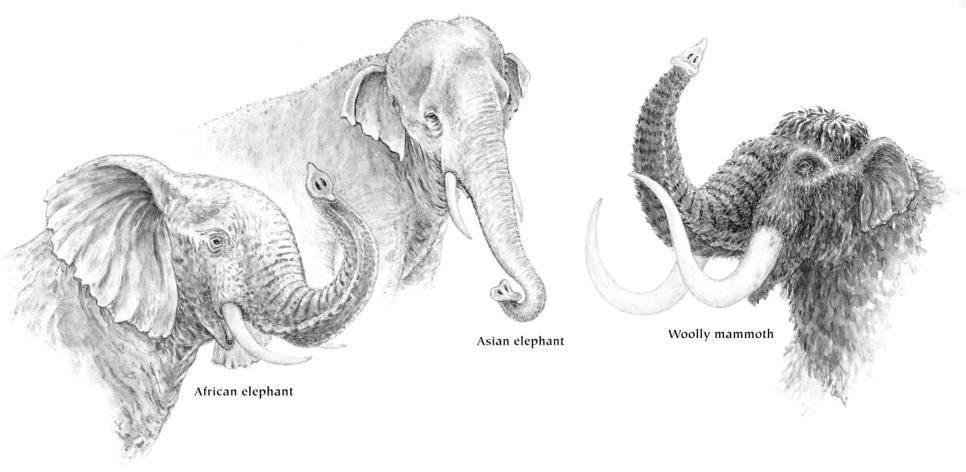

African elephant

Asian elephant

Woolly mammoth

The Elephantidae are part of a larger group of animals called the Proboscidea (pro-BOS-ki-dee-uh), a name that comes from a Greek word meaning long, flexible snout. One of the unique features of elephants and mammoths is the trunk. The trunk is formed by a combination of the upper lip and nose, which over millions of years became extremely long and specialized. Elephants use their trunks for breathing, smelling, touching, picking up things, and making loud trumpeting noises. They bring food and water to their mouths with them and sometimes squirt water over their bodies for a shower bath. No doubt, mammoths used their trunks in much the same way.

The tip of the trunk has one or two fingerlike projections for grasping and holding small objects. The African elephant has two of these projections, whereas the Asian elephant has only one. The tip of the woolly mammoth's trunk had one short and one long projection. The appearance of the tip of the Columbian mammoth's trunk is unknown.

Teeth and Tusks

Like elephants today, mammoths were plant eaters and had four large teeth in their jaws. As the teeth became worn by chewing, they moved forward in the mouth, fell out, and were replaced by a new set. Each succeeding tooth was larger than the one before it. A mammoth could have up to six sets of teeth during its lifetime, with the last set growing in at about age forty-three. After this sixth set finally wore out, the mammoth would die of starvation. Mammoths could live to be sixty or more. Scientists can examine fossil teeth as a way of determining how old the animal was when it died.

Tusks are actually very large teeth. They are the equivalent of the incisors, or biting teeth, in other animals. Tusks grow throughout an animal's lifetime and produce growth rings that show the animal's age and reveal clues to its health. With mammoths, as with elephants, the two tusks grow out of the upper jaw. Like baby elephants, baby mammoths grew a pair of short tusks, about two inches long. These "baby tusks" fell out when the mammoth was a year old and were replaced by permanent tusks.

A single mammoth tooth can be a foot long! Each tooth is constructed of a series of flat, vertical plates that appear as stripes, or ridges, on the tooth's surface. The top of each of these ridges is covered by a layer of enamel.

One Columbian mammoth had tusks 16 feet 5 inches long—one and a half times longer than the longest known elephant tusk. The average weight for a pair of mammoth tusks was 300 pounds, but some weighed 360 pounds or more. Strong muscles in the mammoth's neck and back supported the enormous weight of the tusks. Like elephants today, mammoths probably used their tusks for defense and as tools. With their tusks, the animals could knock over trees, dig holes to find water or minerals, and possibly crack ice to get at food or water.

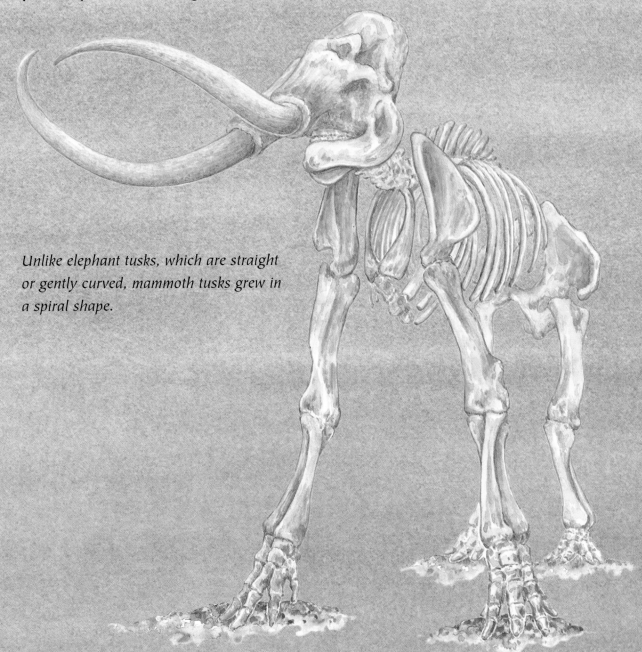

Unlike elephant tusks, which are straight or gently curved, mammoth tusks grew in a spiral shape.

13

Woolly Mammoths

The first woolly mammoths lived in Europe about 300,000–500,000 years ago. They roamed the treeless plains at the edges of the vast ice sheets that covered much of the northern hemisphere during the Pleistocene epoch. They ate grass and low shrubs, chewing their food with large ridged teeth. When the ground was covered by snow, they may have used their long tusks to sweep it away and expose the grass below.

Woolly mammoths were well suited to life in a cold climate. Their skin, which grew to an average thickness of 1.2 inches, was covered with a heavy, shaggy coat that helped them stay warm and dry. Three-inch-thick fat deposits under the skin acted as a layer of insulation. A stocky build, small ears, and a short tail also helped conserve body heat. (An animal with less exposed surface area retains more of its body heat.)

An adult woolly mammoth was between nine and eleven feet tall and weighed from four to six tons. It had a high domed head, humped shoulders, and a back that sloped sharply down from the shoulders to the tail. As with other mammoths and elephants, male woolly mammoths were larger than females and had more massive skulls and thicker tusks.

Woolly mammoths gradually spread across Europe and Asia. About 100,000 years ago, woolly mammoths migrated from Asia into North America across a land bridge that is now the Bering Strait. Fossil remains of woolly mammoths have been found in Alaska, Canada, and the northern United States. Woolly mammoths and Columbian mammoths may have met where their territories overlapped.

A woolly mammoth's coat consisted of a soft, dense undercoat with hairs between two and five inches long and an outer layer of coarse hairs that could be as much as twenty inches long. The color varied from light brown to dark reddish brown to nearly black. The hair of a baby mammoth was softer and more fluffy than that of an adult.

Columbian Mammoths

Columbian mammoths were not as well adapted to the cold as the woolly mammoths, and they lived in warmer, more southerly regions of North America. The Columbian mammoths roamed the grasslands and forests of what is now the continental United States and Mexico. Their fossil bones have been found as far south as Costa Rica.

The Columbian mammoths were the largest land animals of their time and grew to heights of thirteen feet and weights of ten tons. They were distinguished by enormous curling tusks, which sometimes reached lengths of more than sixteen feet. No preserved carcasses of the Columbian mammoth have been found, so we don't have any examples of their skin or hair. Because they lived in a relatively mild climate, however, they probably did not have coats as heavy as those of the woolly mammoths.

All mammoths had big appetites. Based on the daily food intake of an elephant, it is estimated that a single Columbian mammoth ate about seven hundred pounds of food a day. Clues to the diet of the Columbian mammoth were found at Bechan Cave in southern Utah in a huge pile of preserved mammoth dung. Some of the ball-shaped droppings were nearly eight inches across. Dissections of the dung revealed that the animals ate mainly grass and low-growing plants, but that they also fed on the leaves of bushes and trees.

Mastodons

Mastodons were large trunked animals distantly related to mammoths and elephants. These forest dwellers had jagged teeth that were good for eating twigs, leaves, branches, and roots. Mastodons were descendants of an ancient proboscidean group that had its beginnings about 40 million years ago in Africa and then spread throughout the northern hemisphere. Mastodons first appeared about 20 million years ago. They lived in North America from at least 3.75 million years ago until the end of the Ice Age. Mastodons in Europe and Asia became extinct in the early Pleistocene.

The American mastodon, *Mammut americanum* (MAM-mut a-mare-ih-KAN-um), stood about ten feet tall at the shoulder. Its curving tusks grew up to nine feet in length. Preserved patches of skin show that it had a thick coat of reddish brown hair. Its range was from Alaska to Florida, and its fossils are so common that scientists think that the animals must have once roamed the continent in huge numbers. The American mastodon is part of a group known as the gomphotheres (GOM-foe-theers). Several different kinds of gomphotheres lived in South America. They were the only proboscideans to have ever lived on that continent.

MAMMOTH FOSSILS

We know more about mammoths than about any other extinct Ice Age mammals because of the abundance and variety of their fossil remains. Fossils can tell us when and where an animal lived, its age, sex, and size, and sometimes the cause of death. Mammoths died from starvation, disease, accidents, and attacks by predators. Adult mammoths were safe from most predators because of their size, but young mammoths were preyed upon by meat eaters such as lions, wolves, hyenas, and sabertooth cats.

The age of a mammoth bone can be determined in a number of ways, but the most common method is radiocarbon dating. Radioactive carbon is formed in the upper atmosphere when cosmic rays bombard nitrogen atoms. The radioactive carbon combines with oxygen to form carbon dioxide, which is used by plants to produce energy. When an animal such as a mammoth eats a plant, the radioactive carbon becomes part of its body. (Meat eaters get the radioactive carbon when they eat the flesh of plant-eating animals.) Radioactive carbon gradually changes back to nitrogen at a fixed rate. By comparing the amount of radioactive carbon to the amount of normal carbon in a sample, scientists can tell when the plant or animal died. After 5,730 years about half of the radioactive carbon has disappeared. After 45,000 years it is all gone. For fossils older than this, scientists can measure changes in other radioactive elements that have longer "lives."

Discovering Mammoths

Paleontologists often go looking for fossils, but mammoth remains are frequently discovered by accident as well. In 1988, in eastern Utah, workers repairing a dam uncovered the nearly complete skeleton of a sixty- to seventy-year-old male mammoth that had apparently died when it became trapped in a bog. In 1994, construction workers near Grangeville, Idaho, drained a small lake and discovered the bones of several mammoths embedded in the bottom. In the North Sea, fishermen drag nets along the ocean floor to catch bottom-dwelling fish. Along with the fish, their nets regularly bring up fossils of mammoths and other Ice Age animals, including woolly rhinos, reindeer, and giant deer, which roamed this region when the seabed was dry land.

For centuries, people who live in the far north have found mammoth remains buried in the frozen soil. Most often they find skeletons and tusks. Occasionally, though, they find whole bodies. At least twenty-five woolly mammoths have been found frozen in the permafrost of Siberia and Alaska. Frozen carcasses give us an amazing amount of detail about the appearance and body structure of woolly mammoths. Undigested food in the stomach and sometimes even bits of food stuck between the teeth can tell us exactly what the mammoth was eating just before it died.

Ivory hunters have been collecting fossil mammoth tusks in Siberia for centuries. Mammoth ivory is used for making objects ranging from billiard balls and piano keys to jewelry and figurines. It is darker and slightly coarser than elephant ivory, but otherwise similar in quality. So many mammoths once lived in Siberia that some people estimate there are millions of tusks and skeletons still waiting to be found.

Frozen in Time

In 1997, the frozen body of an adult woolly mammoth was discovered in Siberia by two members of a nomadic reindeer-herding tribe. While hunting on the tundra, they noticed a giant tusk sticking out of the ground. They found another tusk next to it, buried just below the surface. The hunters took the tusks to a local market, where they met a French explorer named Bernard Buigues. He persuaded the hunters to take him to the place where the rest of the body still lay, buried in the frozen ground. Preliminary studies showed that the animal was a forty-seven-year-old male and that it had died 22,000 years ago. Buigues recognized the importance of the find and organized an expedition to dig out the mammoth. It was named the Jarkov mammoth after the reindeer hunters who found it.

One of the problems with excavating animals that have been frozen a long time is that as soon as the flesh is thawed, it begins to rot. So instead of thawing the mammoth where it was found, Buigues and his team decided to excavate the carcass as a giant frozen block. They did this in the fall of 1999. After transporting the block by helicopter to the closest town, they placed it in a large ice cave, where it could be slowly thawed and studied. The carcass is providing scientists with a unique opportunity to examine the body tissues of an adult woolly mammoth by using the most up-to-date scientific techniques. Along with the mammoth remains they will also study plants, pollen, and other buried evidence to learn about the mammoth's world.

The Jarkov mammoth's tusks were reattached to the frozen carcass before it was moved.

Baby Mammoths

As with elephants today, female mammoths had their first babies, called calves, when they were in their early teens. The pregnancy lasted about twenty-two months. A newborn mammoth was about three feet tall and weighed about two hundred pounds. Youngsters grew slowly and needed the protection of the herd until they were big enough to look after themselves. Males stayed with the herd until they were about ten years old, whereas females remained with the herd for the rest of their lives. Females reached their full adult size at about the age of twenty-five, and males at the age of forty.

Our knowledge of the various species of baby mammoths comes from fossil bones and frozen carcasses of woolly mammoths. The most famous of these, called Baby Dima, was discovered in 1977 by gold miners in Siberia. As they washed away the top layer of soil to get at the gold-bearing sediments below, they uncovered the body of a male woolly mammoth between six and twelve months old. He was 42 inches tall, 46 inches long, and would have weighed 220–250 pounds when alive. The young calf had died 40,000 years ago after falling into a crevasse or a pool, or possibly by becoming stuck in a bog or mud. His body had been quickly covered and was almost perfectly preserved. Dima's heart was in such good condition that scientists have used it to create a three-dimensional computer image of a mammoth heart. The image shows that the heart chambers and arteries were larger than those of a similar-size elephant, perhaps an adaptation that helped mammoths survive cold weather. An analysis of Dima's blood cells indicates that they were similar to those of an Asian elephant. Frozen mammoth tissues, such as those from Baby Dima, are helping scientists to better understand how a mammoth's body worked.

A Deadly Sinkhole

Since 1974, when fossilized mammoth bones were first discovered near the town of Hot Springs, South Dakota, scientists have unearthed thousands of bones. It is the largest known accumulation of primary mammoth fossils. (Primary fossils are fossils located in the place where the animal died.) Most of the mammoth bones at Hot Springs are the remains of Columbian mammoths, but a few belong to their relatives, the woolly mammoths. Scientists have also found the bones of other smaller animals such as wolves, mice, and prairie dogs.

Nearly all the mammoth fossils are of young males between the ages of eleven and twenty-nine. As with young male elephants, these mammoths would have been newly independent from their mothers' herds. Young males tend to wander alone or in small groups, and without experienced older animals to guide them, they sometimes get into trouble.

The fossils at Hot Springs are of animals that lived about 26,000 years ago. At that time the site was a large sinkhole. (A sinkhole forms when the earth above an underground cave collapses.) A study of the mammoth tusks at Hot Springs shows that all the animals died in winter. Scientists think that the hungry young males were tempted by the green plants that grew year-round next to the hot spring at the bottom of the sinkhole. The mammoths, not aware of the danger of descending into the pit, went down—and never came back. The number of bones found at this site is providing scientists with a unique opportunity to compare specimens and gives a detailed window on the 300- to 700-year time period in which the animals lived.

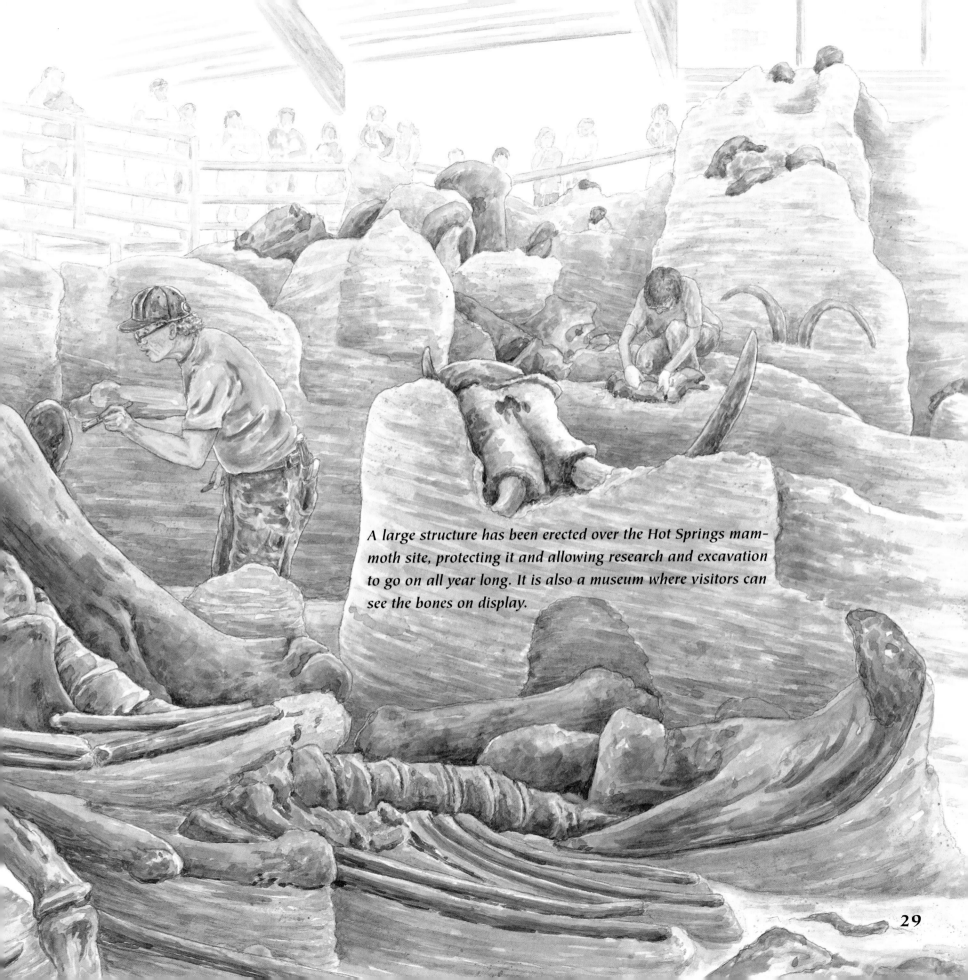

A large structure has been erected over the Hot Springs mammoth site, protecting it and allowing research and excavation to go on all year long. It is also a museum where visitors can see the bones on display.

Trapped in Tar

Toward the end of the last Ice Age, Columbian mammoths, mastodons, sabertooth cats, giant ground sloths, and many other now extinct large animals roamed the hills and flatlands that are the city of Los Angeles today. We know about these animals because their bones were preserved in a place called the La Brea Tar Pits.

Large deposits of oil lie underneath the ground in southern California. In some places the oil seeps upward through cracks in the Earth's crust and forms pools of asphalt, or tar. Sometimes the surface of the asphalt is hidden by leaves or a layer of water. If an animal steps there, its feet become stuck. Unable to free itself from the thick asphalt, the animal dies and its bones eventually sink. Thousands of Ice Age animals, including more than thirty mammoths, became trapped in these asphalt pools.

The fossils of the La Brea Tar Pits were first discovered about one hundred years ago by people who were digging out the tar to use for waterproofing roofs. Since then, scientists have excavated millions of bones. So many animals met their death in the tar seeps that their bones are often jumbled together—like a large, sticky jigsaw puzzle. Besides mammals and birds, the remains of lizards, snakes, turtles, toads, frogs, fish, clams, snails, insects, and spiders have been found. Plants and trees have also been preserved. The huge number of fossils discovered at the La Brea Tar Pits has enabled scientists to develop a detailed picture of the mammoth's world in southern California 10,000–40,000 years ago. At that time, the climate was wetter and cooler than it is today, and it supported a diverse plant and animal community. You can see the assembled skeleton of a Columbian mammoth and those of many other Ice Age animals at the George C. Page Museum in Los Angeles.

Dwarf Mammoths

In 1993, Russian scientists working on a remote island north of the Arctic Circle discovered some amazing fossil bones. They were of a mammoth that probably weighed less than a ton—the size of a youngster—yet all the features were those of a full-grown adult.

Fossils of dwarf mammoths have been found in two places: Wrangel Island, north of Siberia, and the Channel Islands off the coast of California. Thousands of years ago, groups of mammoths migrated to these places, either by crossing frozen water or by swimming. There they established themselves—but when the ice sheets began to melt and ocean levels rose, they became isolated from the rest of the world. In response to a limited food supply and a lack of predators, succeeding generations of mammoths on these islands became smaller and smaller until all the individuals had become dwarfs, or miniature versions, of the species. Those on Wrangel Island were dwarf woolly mammoths, while those on the Channel Islands

were dwarf Columbian mammoths. The smaller animals needed less food, and there was no need for large body size as a defense against predators. Like other mammoths, the miniature mammoths eventually became extinct, although those on Wrangel Island lasted until about 3,500 years ago—surviving longer than mammoths anywhere else in the world. The fossils of the dwarf mammoths of Wrangel Island and the Channel Islands are especially interesting to scientists because they provide a record of how a species can change dramatically over a relatively short period of time.

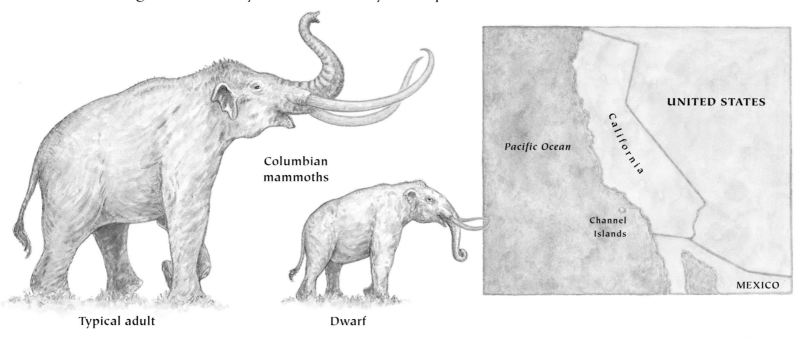

Columbian
mammoths

Typical adult

Dwarf

UNITED STATES

Pacific Ocean

California

Channel
Islands

MEXICO

Woolly
mammoths

Wrangel Island

SIBERIA

ALASKA

Bering Sea

Dwarf

Typical adult

PEOPLE AND MAMMOTHS

In the Dordogne region of southern France, there are passageways deep in Rouffignac cave that stretch for miles. More than 15,000 years ago, prehistoric humans decorated the walls with hundreds of images, including more than 150 depictions of woolly mammoths. In one long tunnel, two groups of painted mammoths appear to parade in a line, their leaders meeting head to head. In another, a drawing engraved in the rock shows the hairs of the mammoth's woolly coat reaching almost to the ground.

People began picturing mammoths in their art as early as 30,000 years ago. Except for horses, mammoths are the most frequently pictured animal in prehistoric art. Most of the four hundred known images of mammoths are found in Europe or the Ural Mountain region on the border of Europe and Asia, but a few pictures of mammoths are carved in rock walls in the western United States.

More than half the known cave drawings of mammoths are found at Rouffignac, France. This mammoth's image, which was carved into the cave wall, is two feet seven inches high and four feet long.

Using Tusks and Bones

Prehistoric people used mammoth tusks and bones for making art objects, tools, and furniture, and sometimes even for building houses. Objects made of mammoth ivory include beads, bracelets, spoons, and needles. In eastern Europe, archaeologists have found the remains of more than seventy huts constructed of mammoth bones and tusks. Bones and tusks must have been plentiful, providing good building material in places where there were few trees. Heat for the huts came from fire pits dug in the floor, and charred mammoth bones indicate that these were used as fuel. Once ignited, the bones would have burned well.

It is likely that people ate mammoth meat, at least on occasion. In a number of places, stone tools found alongside mammoth fossils indicate that people had cut meat off the bones. Although prehistoric people had spears that they could have used to kill mammoths, it is not certain that they hunted them. Instead, they may have scavenged meat from recently dead animals or taken advantage of any weak or injured animals that they found.

A group of mammoth bone huts were constructed about 15,000 years ago at a place called Mezhirich in Ukraine.